# MASQUE

# MASQUE

Elena Karina Byrne

TUPELO PRESS
*Dorset, Vermont*

## ACKNOWLEDGMENTS

Versions of these poems appeared in the following journals:

*Agenda* (UK): "Master & Servant: Mask"; "Your Death Mask"; "Mask of Artifice"; "Animal Mask"; "Narcissism: Rorschach Mask"; "A Weightless Mask: Light"

*American Poetry Review*: "Paraphrase: Paper Mask"; "Mask of Marie Antoinette"

*Colorado Review*: "Doppelganger Mask: Double Accusative"

*Chelsea*: "Misrule Mask: The Abbot of Unreason"; "Sex Mask"; "Mirror's Mask"; "First Kiss: An Italian Mask"; "*Sturm und Drang* Mask"; "Ventriloquist's Mask"

*Denver Quarterly*: "Blessing Mask: Night"; "Between the Divide: Invisible Mask"

*Fireweed*: "Enough Mask"

*Heartstone*: "Mask of Flowers"

*Hotel Amerika*: "Due North: Mask"

*Onthebus*: "Orphan Mask"

*Painted Bride Quarterly*: "Vanquish Mask: 9th Century Japan"

*Paris Review*: "Dogma Mask in Favor of Alice"; "Magritte's Mask"

*Ploughshares*: "Queequeg's Tattoos: A Headless Mask"

*Prairie Schooner*: "Fertility Mask"; "Wedding Mask"

*Poems & Plays*: "Face Mask: The Art of Physiognomy"

*Pool*: "Manifest Destiny: Flying"

*Rivendale*: "Anesthesia Mask"

*Solo*: "Mask of Insomnia"

*Snake Nation*: "Lying Mask"; "History of Restoration: Grief Mask"; "Necropolis War Mask: A Bearer of Two Faces"

*Tebot Bach Anthology*: "Paradise Mask"

*The Journal*: "Rant Mask"

*The Los Angeles Review*: "Irregular Masks"

*TriQuarterly*: "Disguise Mask"; "She Mask: Inversion"

*Valley of Contemporary Poets Anthology*: "Vertigo Mask"; "Phantom Mask"

*Volt*: "Of Measure: Mask"

*Verse*: "Spring Mask"

*Yale Review*: "Moon Mask"

"Irregular Masks" also appears in *The Best American Poetry 2005*

Portions of "Sex Mask" appear in *Spunk & Bite: A Writer's Guide to Punchier, More Engaging Language & Style*, by Arthur Plotnik, Random House Reference, 2005

**TABLE OF CONTENTS**

This book is for my Peter, Dylan, and Chloe...

My unending thanks to my publisher, the marvelous poet Jeffrey Levine. Thank you tireless Tupelo Press staff!

For the purity of revelation, love and inspiration, my darling, brilliant Cathy Colman.

My love to those in blood, near and far: my mother Marcia S. Jepson, my brother Stephen, Nick and David, Serena and Jeffrey, and of course, my father Herbert S. Jepson, and Lynne, no longer with us.

This is also for our dear Agha Shahid Ali, because one must never forget.

Again, and again, for constant support and friendship, an ignited Thank You! for David St. John, Galway Kinnell, Brigit P. Kelly, Molly Bendall, Kathy Fagan, Angie Estes, Forrest Gander, Susan McCabe, Brendan Constantine, Kelli Noftle, Gail Wronsky, Marty Williams, Teresa Carmody, Vanessa Place, Ilya Kaminsky, Gabriel Meyer, Stuart Dischell, Cecilia Wolloch, Dana Levin, Tess Gallagher, Lynne Emanuel, Thomas Lux, Jeffrey Vasseur, Sherod Santos, Bill Wadsworth, Jay McCulloch, Christopher Merrill, Stephanie Brown, Karen Sexton-Josephs, JoEllen Williamson, Donna Prinzmetal, Brenda V. Finch, Camie Laine, David Phelps, Donald Bell, Noah Blaustein, Arthur Plotnik, Timothy Dansdill, Randall Watson and Lawrence Bridges.

Thank you Alfredo de Palchi and Chelsea magazine for an unexpected embrace.

Thank you artist Ann Hamilton for her recent communication, her images over the years, her body-object series, the self portraits paying homage to the averted self, camouflage, a portrait participating in language, the self embodying interior movement, and finally a true vertigo of seeing, where we come to "a border, a threshold, a place that's in between," and how you "feel through your body, you take in the world through your skin."

*I made your image wear different masks,*
*and I played with it nightly and in my dreams.*
*I took your mask and put it on other faces*
*which looked as if they might know you.*

—Sylvia Plath


Yes, I doubled you tonight.

Your stolen hope of my skin. Who you are in resemblance to you.

This ode-angst, if only it were arugula, Italy in the dark, the gondola

    filled with green lilies like your lungs.

But it's not.

    More like the peeping Tom's keyhole to this universe, vicarious

thinking

    which goes unpunished.

There is no love or hate without a face.

*De nobis fabula narratur : their story is our story*

and so it goes. And so I look

for you in the livelihood of dreaming, draw you in

so close

my circulation is cut off, gossip knot tied too tight, close

    enough to recognize you in the beforehand.

When discourse was disguise, I carried your likeness

in those other faces.

So speak

to me, your spellbind just might get a message across

    my mouth.


What I can't say in return won't hurt

you. Speak book-backwards

    so I can read you in another language, then

I will put you on, out-

        numbered by expressions on the expressionless.

A mask for each body part, to fit the hands and feet

                looking up at me.


    A kind of devotional

quarantine, a snuff of the past

which now looks like anyone's future. But it's mine

    you're looking at; I am your only addict

        and I solemnly share you, your visceral ruin, a variation

on the pale mask I pass around. Don't you see? Here:

    I take your face seriously.

If I can't have you, everyone else will.

*In relation to each other men are like irregular verbs in*
*different languages; nearly all verbs are slightly irregular.*

—Kierkegaard

They had beaten their heads against the walls of waves
    until a thousand green fish glittered to the surface,

had drawn your inside thigh-blood, silent
    for a slow pint at the neighborhood pub,

with their hair trailing behind them, had fled all bad
    words hung from the attic rafters overnight,—

still those who, singing, had begun masturbating their way
    back to original sin, or thousands, born

to alcoholics, with sorrow as large as houseboats, have
    drunk the hand-wash of airport pickpockets,

and others blindfolded by luck, caught the hurricane's eye
    to move in with the summer storm's shearing, for

another who has burst the helium balloon you bore in mind
    like a glow-in-the-dark apple the doctor gave away:

oh, how many more have broadcast, breakneck, their own
    breathing, told the moon it was the sleeper's open mouth

in the outskirts of the city, who have fallen to their knees
    to see the shape of the world on the back of a baby's head

with those, serious, knowing real consequence was a matter
    of verb tense's wear and tear on the past, that no two

faces are the same, just like any stunned Vermont snowflake father said,
    disappearing easy as its memory, once it reached your skin…

## PARAPHRASE: PAPER MASK

*Your head unrocking to a pulse, already*
*Hollowed by air, posts a white paraphrase*
*Among bruised roses on a peppered wall.*

—Hart Crane


This one was presented to me
while I was falling asleep:—Papier Mache wall, veil of paraphrase
from the words you sent, from the perishing stanzas in the bed,
to assume this air-appearance, one bruised shadow
on the new white paper, skin of God, letter, simple sum
of both our voices.


I was speaking from the mask
with the tongue of pearls:
        my breath softened this compromise
and the edges of the mask.
I wore all the extravagance of lost syllables.
I was sleeping on paper.
I was speaking from the tapestried books of Eros, speaking

to your wrists. It was the pulse
        of dying bees, pale in a bowl,
carried across a dry field.

The sky was a blank page of the mask.
Bees: this terrifying
devotion to language.

*Simple though Malay sex was, it had an abundant vocabulary.*
*To copulate was jamah or berjima or juma'at or bersatu*
*(literally to become one), or sa-tuboh, asmara, beranchok (this*
*term was peculiar to Perak), ayut, ayok and much, much more.*

—Anthony Burgess


Can I, for a moment?

Dada you to accord something light
first, sweet you and slow
you as a canoe, to window you and murmur
you, to revoke your thinking
from under your hands, counterpart your legs
before you sinew and quayside over my cry for more,
spreading my hidden quilting unstitched, compulsive
to desk your posture and arm your surrender, reveling
what we ornament in case
we bedstead and double-dutch and exact,
cashier our way in deeper, brulee the making time
to another breast, birthday the bones
that have lost their weight, to become
the earned work, ass, generous habit
and fierce illuminating breath, to world
our countries back, bend and weaken,
for ceaseless-keeping entrances
to the extravagance, habitual the belly down to
the dissolve and gospel the frequency, burn
the confetti narrative now, now impatience
past thinking, oh, or patience
your abandon, itself surrender as preserve
audience and alive, unlikely to longer or
to festival you extra time again
and release under exile, oh
to devotion, to vowel and palette or
fidelity our volition, name again
that it must precede this kiss in part
and whole matter over the give and take
of the body, one body, even
more words…

## BEE MASK

*The queen bee marries the winter of your year.*

—Sylvia Plath

Your bleached headdress for the garden, closed-in
canvas canopy and gossamer shield
keeps them just away.         Word-away.

Sweet enough. Swooned
hovering in their swarm:
the dizzy worker bees like small indecisions
float their anvils over the air, trying
to find the open flowers

of your ears.        Strange vernacular.

You sleep-out these margin cargoes of light, tinted
holograms.

The engine, the box hive, keeps new time
and the headmask, like a fallen ghost of an archangel
refuses to see.        Now, flying is outright
falling,—like the voice swaying over.

But don't speak.

Bees duplicate enough rage
when following the Queen.
What other sound forgives the beginning of each minute?

Listen:

You come to the ground's frenzied confessions
knitted from so many fresh blossoms.    Here,
you will always know April
and every hour's almost up where the beekeeper
explains your name, down the very

path of doubt.

Nihil nos celat *(Nothing us conceals-he: 'He conceals nothing from us').*
—*The Oxford Companion to the English Language*

You think giving away
envy, you give people what they want,
give them the face on a platter, badass double,
terror's vertebrae, sparing yourself nothing
safe from speed, a kind of hands-on performance, Jack's
ripper-disposition and laughter you picked out
of a crowd as hell's better half
cut from the same cloth, or charitable mirror's mercury,
linguists' long vowel trampled and
palate's tongue tied to its needy twin?

Lautrec's women wade the dry shoreline while
the national average changes.
Vice is all we need right now, a bigger craving
for greed, the hot water we get ourselves into.
There's always evidence of an enemy, a lack of manners
when you come. You or is it I? I closed my eyes once
and started again without default. I took disobedience

as a way of life, a fiction behind the driver's seat saving
obscenities and jism; I took you
for granted, dear ghost next door, double-goer, everlasting
grace coming up for air
behind me. You were wearing daybreak
and one hand over your eye. You were
everything I expected from a lack of discipline
and decade of good looks.

I waive my right to keep coming back
to you. I am all Belfast and DNA now,
the book thrown at you
for the next time you try to take
the back seat and the next time you think
life isn't the nearest thing to life
you can get.

## MIRROR'S MASK

> *...the mirror image is a Firstness already anchored to a*
> *Secondness insofar as it establishes a necessary and direct*
> *relation between the mirroring and the thing being mirrored.*
>
> —Umberto Eco, from *Kant and the Platypus*


I am always awake, alive in refraction, the narrative
switchblade, shining.

> I can use all my intrusive powers
> because I can dare any dark
> to bring you to the table; this is not a drunken exchange—
> it is the truth
> explaining itself to your face
> for me.

Impoverished by no one,      I am
perfect congruency, liquid light
losing my head
for the absolute proper noun that is you.

Every first false impression, cynical offer
of silver, even the silver lining.

> Watch,      I'll absorb you
> like an underwater air bubble
> and give you away every time.
> I am your vicarious surrogate setting you free
> like a tattoo on your sex, my
> perfect correspondence to your face, first.

But my lust is terrifying because it never really knows
you.   Only so far to reflection,
smell the mercury, split the second
it takes to take your visage back. Now.     See me
and say your name:

You look good from here, looking
me in the eye, receiving.
I have saved your image,
bitten-back by context, disenchanting
and necessary. I will never die nor
pick you out of a crowd.     Second sight,

you will always come on your own
accord to me. So,
when you do, cover this face in dead blue moths
that will move when you speak,     then bend down,
down close, close, and cheat on me,—over me,

lightly breathe
for me.

# VANQUISH MASK: 9th CENTURY JAPAN

okashi, *a smile suddenly expressed and quickly gone.*
—Bradley Smith, *Japan, a History in Art*


"You cannot break my breath," she says, "being at last
breath."          Concealed
by cloud, cursive dissolve, her face
                    is made of *gofun*, the crushed aged oyster shell, white
powder pigment and perfection.
                    Light sent adrift
on the wish to be like air, winter will come
composed of the breadash she carries in her sleeves.

There are no burdens of joy.
What might be invented is as
disconsolate & unrehearsed as devotion.

She sees him
from the inside of the mask. She's accurate
lament, daughter of animal glue & sawdust, daughter
of paper & grass doll sent adrift on the river.

"You cannot see past this," she accuses
in one gesture over her head
toward the windows.

Haunts to keep still: *respiration, respiration…*

She likes all talcum sounds before words.
She likes to whisper at night
because you can see the face better.

# NECROPOLIS WAR MASK: A BEARER OF TWO FACES

*I want a touch of bitterness in everything–always*
*a jeer in the midst of our triumphs, desolation even*
*in the midst of enthusiasm.*

—Gustave Flaubert

But let me multiply by you.
I have your hieroglyph number here
deep in my mouth. There:
penetrate my psyche until you can't see
straight. This is, after all, the blood-century again.
My own head is ready to fall into a basket
of horse straw. The sky is still outside. Cracking
under my own pressure, I am all fervor and painstaking,
toughing-out winter, fit for consumption,
red berry skin and thorn, rejecting battle scars
because no war makes us who we are not.
Melee to my future, you
are penning an impersonator with no mercy
but I know all your bad habits
and I've read my rights, so please
try to convince me I am not you. I will surrender
nothing, but will scrub this face painting-pale
so you can see me better. Save face
for us both. Then lie for me. I'll make your distance
my proximity beyond the pale, the better
boundary. The world will scare
a fascist elegy out of you,
the question not asked. Word for word.
even in this midst,
there are whole days
I brain and brawl and borrow back
an abundance of words troubling for water.
There are whole days
I am thirsty at night.
You see: the time lapses here in our own arms.
Now break your silence; tell me a story I can't stand.

## STURM UND DRANG MASK

> *...late eighteenth-century German literature was trying*
> *to free itself from French influence.*
>
> —Josefa H. Byrne, *Mrs. Byrne's Dictionary of*
> *Unusual, Obscure and Preposterous Words*


This is territorial now: close the gates.

Expel all soft syllables and slaves, God with his domain
of insults and family silver.
Get out the buckets and sex toys. A storm is coming,
brewing and billowing a blue-black cloud

our way. Give me the liberty of words
and memorable watermarks on the soil.        Give
me the tendency to be my own tyrant, give me the time of day
when light is a stranger asking for food at our door.
Everything is empire here. We can squander
what we know best, break the crude spell of the calendar
for something a little more passionate and our own.

I know I am heavy-handed like this.
The disproportionate picture pulled from the black lake.
The shape of the last breath in my mouth. I know I want
to make a move, unmoored. Water reeds my hair, your hands part of
my body. But there's no going back.
I am qualified to give myself a new name. Implicit
display of bad temper. Revolt tourniquet flag tied around
your thigh. I am Werther's sorrow.
Let no sanity save me.        Hurry. Send this letter

to the Solitude Palace in Stuttgart first, then on to France.
I can only imagine what you're going to have to do with me next.

*Oh! How foul a thing, that we should see the*
*tongue of one animal in the guts of another.*

—Leonardo da Vinci, *The Notebooks, 1295*


Oh! More than me, twice, I am.
Twofold, of two minds.
I am inside the mask made of blue corn husks.
Where else
can I begin in such significance, my own worn element?

Bend the need to yield; rust the hours.
Acquiesce our duplicate pleasure,—corruptible
as incorrigible, but this is only

　　　the appearance of confinement, insolent and lacquered.
What we have wanted from each other
all along: an inseparable, same face.
Our vanity is irrational.

Wake me. Tell me what to do with myself in the dark.
Our life is made of words. The world obeys
no apology. Here

I demand your full attention
and a tied locket of your hair.

Your being,　my nothing.

## ORPHAN MASK

*L'etat, c'est moi*

—Louise XIV


No, I am the State,
scaled down to size, a double
indemnity, a geranium
in the dry fist of winter.

Dear Kindness,
do not come looking for me. It is too late. I cannot tame what is
     about to happen.
You see, one dreams the territorial, dreams someone has your story,
     shares a perversion for oversized rooms and high ceilings
but has no home, no idle realm, nor lasting digression. I love a god
alone like me, swinging from his hammock, his black
mouth open with a real despair for stars, a convert companion
who collects anchors and maps, squanders cheating, spits shiny
watermelon seeds into the little coffin paper beds
     of the empty chocolate box,
a self-punishment for knowing no one. And because the broken
scullery is filled with strychnine in tins, wallpaper-smothered cornflowers
sealed in arsenic who say, Yes, I say, Yes, but cannot return the favor.

So: To temper
this rush-blood feeling inherited at birth
I place my every seal in red
wax, my signature
and no domain air down. Leave me now.
You know
I have handmade work to do: ragged
heirloom, chromosome ruin,
and mournful prophecy memory.
Because, there will be
no unjust space
big enough for me.

14

*…space-time…a priori forms of sensibility…If the whole world were reduced to a single glove, it would still have to be a right or a left glove, and this, intelligence alone will never understand.*

—Immanuel Kant


I cannot, anyway, choose.
You're right,—
        *there's no one world*, no two
or three taken. I am proof
in the hand-persimmon, raw
undomesticated chance the knife will be used. We are
single glove.
Align your side. Only you

                can suggest skin at this point
of departure. We let the knife remain
in the sink. It returns light's perpetuity
by chrome. Out of context,
        this dark slide
        comes with a silver opening
by blade, a kind of seeing as the edge
        of the universe disturbs my head.

Where shall I offer the intimate benevolence of the first
clean cut?

      Now all syllables are stressed, you see. In the beforehand.
But my body will always be
        unrehearsed. Close up: gleam.
I am a person of color, of no color, language, no religion, region…
Offstage, on the street, at a greater-than
        distance to you.

Move back, further.

Tell me the only truth.

## MASK OF MARIE ANTOINETTE

*My Sister*
*I am writing to you for the very last time.*

—Marie Antoinette

I cannot repeat from my own invention of what I am, that I am not myself and therein more, through everything I trust to leave, in this heart-wrenching condemned-minded promise, but leaving, *I am calm, as one always is when one's conscience is clear*, the sky's monarchy opening up above me as evidence, and if my body be this fruited apology to their treason, how easy it is to speak and not be understood, how easy a confession to being alive, heedless love, how easy for all of us. Please, keep this memory and my children close to you, embrace this detour and reason so I have not squandered my inaugural north, nor opposed, even against my own inevitable ghost-face, the rocky coastline that returns our language to us and to its better ground, better hour than what it was, dear one to my sadness, such pretense that exhausts the immortal, and because we are not without failing omnipotence in our affair of numbers, still together, forgive me, my powerlessness, after me, to know you have received this.

*In the evening I walked sadly along the shore of the Solent, eastwards
by Pylewell—returning, brought home a glow worm and put it in a
white lily, through which it shone.*

—William Allingham, *from his diary. 1863*

You are dying.

A figure of bees defies your winter's tale, inside,
frenzied undulant and exit, a kind
of miraculous free-form pure sex
descending the steep bluff of blackened
anatomy. The lengths we go
to know sorrow.
Like your father's feet, still flawless
and hanging above you from the door-
jammed dream, the cold
inner flanks of dark green skunk weed,
moon's washbasin face.
The canvas
has not been touched or unrolled.
You execute Kumquat pit and persuasive
crimes of nature. The matchmaker
imagines the portrait and its appetite
for synesthesia. Yes,
someone changed grace.
There would be access to the heart
like a nervous mistress.
There would be entire rooms made for swimming.
Whales and one night watchman who welcomes you
to the truth with his teeth.
But someone lied.

Someone told you so.

# THE HISTORY OF RESTORATION: GRIEF MASK

*...and my brush, continuously dripping onto my face*
*turns it to a rich mosaic.*

—Michelangelo, *from a sonnet on himself*
*at work on the Sistine Chapel.*


The French flannel in your hand,
soaked in solution, drips down your raised arm,
round your neck, slipping its tiny wet tongue
between your breasts. The lacquered color
that changed with soot and grease from tallow of altar candles
now comes shocking as the future in front of you.
Your body is contorted, your arms, white, numb.
Everything is slowing down. You'd rather peel potatoes
with your teeth than see yourself smiling among
the people being pulled with you out of the shadow of
the painting. But you want to get back to fail
the silence, humiliated idiom, to remember
the original face spilling out into the room.
The windows are open but you are still running out of air.
Visitors tell you to stay up all night with it, to take
the portrait back to its intended patina,
that all those hours will be forgotten in an instant.
The pain in your legs will be worth it.
You'll have no time to eat because this is an ongoing elegy
to the body dividing its image. How many times
will you clean, salvage, *stato d'animo*,
inhabit the rush of darkness?
Don't you know: destiny has always been
boring, giving you a glimpse of reconciliation?
And you'll admit, the face was a catwalk
out of the past, your own receding pose.
There now, don't despair.
We have always made strangers out of ourselves
by loving others.

*The moon's best lover*

—Hart Crane

White domain.
Black domain.

  Bleached flour and salt of him,
his head hung with paper orchids and goat bells
over the black water, heavy
from the balcony.
Not this King, great
burlap octopus who came out
to see his subjects, the chipped riff-raff
of stars and ignited gas, this scalawag, he
whose reign is loss and umbilical gut-
wrenching desire, no, not him,
whose open-boat skeleton slowly drifts
through the Queen's gate, a great white
glare, unpolished in its welter of stolen light
to the heart's content
from a fisticuffs of distance,
or Varuna with orders for the seasons
riding sea monster by night
to take on the brood elegy of the past
one domino at a time, no, no,
not the monarchy
when the sky was always there, dogma-
dark, not that, not him, but
behind the rule of waves, slipped from
his silver Orphean lock, another face,
tossed coin, a new time
just for you and your pound of flesh,
the sweet exchange made for his mouth
when he comes to you, stripped
of sadness and once royal blood, to bear
his white chest, his unclenched figure of speech

and hold court, making his steep climb
from the unfinished wood chair
to the sky on this *monan dag*, day of the moon,
night of the moon, rising
in his heat, as far as you will know, into
the arms of the perfect you,

perfect stranger.

*A band of young men took advantage of the confusion,*
*the noise, the excitement and gaiety to jump into our*
*automobile, remove our masks and begin kissing us…*

—Anaïs Nin, from *Little Birds*


Look at me,

       I enjoy it.
I have no difficulty with this part of the pose.
                      My body has no weight
where you can see me.

I had to pose for an illustrator once, for a classroom
of art students under the live musk of charcoal and paint, sound
of their hands circling the paper, and it felt as though I had
already been there in another language.
                      I was once bent over
on horseback, an undressed Hindu mystic, Burlesque
dancer, the satin wish of an opened Heian kimono…No one
ever says a word, the room floating and delayed
                      by our silence
and the next day, if we met on the street,
they wouldn't recognize me
in my wakefulness, which would give me pleasure.

Clearly, the face wears its own mask:
                      two women at once,
I am that which is between myself and the viewer.
I am the suspense in the hands
and submission's image drawn down.

                      Perhaps the kiss
never given away…so kiss open
a piece of me

now,—
                      wait for me, anonymous
in the dedicated light, but

cough before you come
so that I know where you are in the room,
and untangle the climbing vine of my name
whenever I am not there
                    to see you do it.

*…My first kiss tasted like the streets of Rome.*
*My first kiss tasted like the swans of Venice. My first word*
*was random gender. My first gender was the streets of my town*
*and walking them was my first kiss.*

—Caroline Crumpacker


Octave of place, in a crowd's din, she placed it on for no one.

Some two hundred years ago, on the streets of Venice's festival,—
someone else wore this gold leather mask, the seamless subtext in silence
and embroidery
            for a kiss, a first taste to taste

in the mouth of a stranger. Now
she escapes no lust, wants the first again, to be the least expectation,
        countering

consciousness with a look. Look
at her mouth, a nest and vowel.

It is the beginning of all gender
and run its course without language cast
                or split consequence.

She is growing to love what we do not know in the exaggeration
of our sex—
and of your jeopardous kiss

through the mask. We couldn't be anywhere else.

Listen, I say
first words are priceless:

pay the pretty penny.

## NARCISSISM: RORSCHACH MASK

> *...if you show someone one of the blots—a well-known one
> that looks like a bat or a butterfly—and he looks at that
> and sees a giraffe, it is not a good sign...*
>
> —Lilienfield, *associate professor of psychology
> at Emory University*

Train-crushed pennies, pretty.
     Without the mirror image, twins whose seams tongue
the ridge of clouds     they are

not angels because angels don't wear       out
their high-heeled red, pomegranate's thin skin sex.
     The tomato's aspic is left.
Say
the last dusk
     put on its face, the oil print on glass,
     but that is no consolation

to being human or hurt by the lover who can't finish
his sentence. This picture
     has been pushed too far. The lupine lost
its nipple

and an empty bowl, its blue. For the first time I can see
     who washed up on shore
     who took the darkness down
          and who invented the tweak in the bad engine.
It's the same person who squeezed you right out of yourself
one cherry at a time.     The stain

for false impressions' dried blood-
letting fleams. Ready to eat, to be eaten. You can't
     see yourself twice. But hunger brings you
back
     to the table, inkblotted, all sugared for argument's sake.

> *my tongue upon your throat—singing*
>
> —Hart Crane

Eyelash, some furtive kissing and the idea
of your body
in my hands, your lily pad heart float, mine,
purple's liver bile, belief
behind anima, this, your umbilical
cord pull, I

                    memorize without touching,

ribs, the oiled waves of each
intestine, bitten fingernails and sweet constant release
of pancreas, every studio's drop of paint, burning
woodchip charcoal singe lace and pituitary sting you try to hide
                  from your untied brain

for me,—I have my tongue upon them to taste.

       To eat of you: those little deaths I crave.
The clusters' blackberries in my eyes will breed and spill
over you until you can't move

any more, words returning and returning
like a sexually familiar blood-tide squeeze, like too many confetti-
              filled balloons in a small room.
             I'll scare it out
of you, croon and coax and counter, to spleen,

how to make you cayenne-dance backwards at
night, yielding only moon, my makeshift to ask you
              to do things: flower, remove your bra
at the dinner table, read Japanese, science yourself to mint, slowly,
and never forget names, the tin
weathervanes above. Write,

         which is what I want, marrow

to this thought, out of you, for me, instead
of me. If Goya had a black ink hand
                        and knife to the back of your neck,
then I would know what to do, upside down because beauty is useless now

like knowing one's own DNA. Yes,
I am garlic to your memory and last lilac, your skin, my
heat under the ass and armpits, every after-smell of cumin, of cum before
        your collarbone, ovary egg and vowel. Now,

the more longing, the better firebox and water-faith, better herb whistle
                        and feel of our tireless libido backbone held up inside,
every affliction seam, sentence-intuition sewn
                        all the way to this
defied afterlife, to the open lungs.          At the *natura* I sound-out


        you, sing wine and see, spit,—leave this country for new words, this
shipwreck splinter and vex, to universe
your endurance and the now, now to silence my chest so you can have a say,
        sleigh-way,

now bittern hair dark, your voice,
a little south, an orange I can dig my nails into: without choice,

                        marathon me here on plate and page. Make me
failing grandeur, conjured. Served for dinner, you're sure
                        to die here
having sex, pudenda-minded, but I insist

not miscast, misnomer or mucilage in
                anyone's heart, no nine goddesses' eyes. Yet, yet resurrect, again,
        desire of me
all the way because you can. Because: fit of abstraction or cogitate brood stew,

                I know you speak to me
for the salty sake of a body's conjugation in loss, to departure, to believe, lisp,
to devour, avalanche, eat          and of course, love
like this.


26

*And who asked springtime*
*for its kingdom of clear air?*

—Pablo Neruda

Deep sleep, glister and minnow, half-
    eaten rose or
last resort, favorite impulse
    place here
covered in cut grass and human ash
    a eucalyptus awning
high over her, where he bore
    in mind (behind)
the hard wind's swing toward her head
    where the garden
was never Eve's, lilac-blackened
    blocking this
light all winter, tight green bud-
    tongues, metallic
taste of early green when she didn't
    know any better
to peel wet petals back with her teeth
    or call the cold
from under all the doors, new stitched faille
    of ice on the windows
veil for face, spider's gauze, failed lasting
    grace, lace hiss
lacking remorse, so that this spring
    can come on
with its clear air and clean earth
    twelve hands
on twelve clocks sweeping the bride's
    hair, her becoming
a paper kite ascending the indecent
    blue of him.

## OF HIM, THIS VERTIGO: BREATH MASK

*If a man breathed a woman's vapor, his breath soul would
be weakened and his mind would become fuzzy and lose its
power to focus on the hunt.*

—Ann Feinup-Riordan,
*The Living Tradition of Yup'ik Masks*

Now her breath.
Now the whole air from her mouth pushed inside his, exhaled hours later
into his hands before going to bed. Now her breath like dropped
pebbles' rings, moving, slow into their own transparency, left on his pillow
as the already unfolding
half-wing of the face, dream-inhale and sexual double notes. Now the
mind is good
measure and what you can't see won't hurt you. Now he's still weak at the edge
of her body and her breathing. Now halfway strange to himself, halfway
apparitional.
Now,
dizzy, he is the undermusic of her speech, all the way down darkness. Now,
the uncut white paper wind. Now the past who inherits them both. Now
the distance between sky and falling, inner ear aria. Now and now, being alive
like that, never contained in vanishing and reoccurring. Now aspiration,
expectation. Now the century's stronghold, lucent circle above their heads.
Now the nothing made of them making sound. Now nothing
he can do.

Now the cliff.
Now her breath.

In my body before, I knew in your mouth before you said it.
I knew it in my dream unfolding like a *darari-obi*, before I felt
it dissolve on my tongue, single ash, every time you touched the wishbone
ear. I felt it before Mesopotamian tile dice and counters, I felt it
no longer separate from us, down the arms as heat, hurrying. I knew it
as saints disrobing before water. I knew it
under the hundred birds' feet
still on the branch, one motion in the brain, lifting. I saw it
in your back against the chair, among all those people, restless-witholding
and I saw it before the night sky crossed its inevitable winter arc,
up close I knew it before you looked at me across the Italian dusk room
and letter-bound before I said it with a 17th century monarchy's privilege
overriding the banquet flowers that I knew appeared pressed on your
eyelids every time you woke with my name, here I knew it when the
birch trees
surrounded the house, changing places with the armed dead.
I saw it sanctioned in all the unchipped crystal glasses put away for the year.
I knew the one thing that changed us
we couldn't have seen coming:

## WEDDING MASK

*—Always this passion for illusion!*

—Goethe, *Mephistopheles in Faust, Part 1*


Candle wax and white flame,
he was nostalgic and had the lost complexion
of deep winter, all devour and devotion.

Ceremonial, she was ready
to sing if she had to, anything
infatuating and misunderstood.
She was the sweet returning temperament of silk
clothes fallen to the floor
he counted on:
mixed with longing's inexorable, the seamless darkness
of the universe, crushed
Victorian blue glass, flower bulbs filled with champagne, dark
peach velvet trim. The succession
of the years was always his assertion.

"Taste here, but don't look this time," she said, offering
the unconditional apologies
of her hands over his body
as the rain overhead made salt
and pepper, pepper
and salt, and pepper
and new snow.

*I am over-run, jungled in my bed, I am infested with a menagerie of desires: my heart is eaten by a dove, a cat scrambles in the cave of my sex, hounds in my head obey a whipmaster who cries nothing but havoc as the hours test my endurance with an accumulation of tortures…How can I find bird-relief in the nest building of day-to-day? Necessity supplies no velvet wing with which to escape. I am indeed and mortally pierced with the seeds of love.*

—Elizabeth Smart

All as in fleeing: it's common law or none
and love, and the animal round in your bowsight you see.

My impropriety obeyed can be visible daily like this: animal
and animal. What peaceable kingdom not had here.

I'm earthwormed behind the skull's beehive curve, a constant
for you, Jack Mackerel's silver swim with no apparent sense, the turned

Cortez Soapfish wash: clean me—and Starry Flounder: eat me—a Bride
of the Sea from Venice with the Canting Crew of beggars, as my own,

their slang-whining speech, the dark dusty mole's groundfall root
and blood which surrounds my heavy head. There's nothing me

like now, supposition's plucked feather, yellow, Minah-eye, crested
and crow-cornered, high, nested too high to see my own creature's

escape, my own Tuvalu's coral atolls' fluorescence, fish-scaled, dissolved
to a tiny goby, nor me, deeper down, the Narwhal's underwater horn.

Shall I put on a happy face, instead human, for you? I do not
redeem the horsehair braid, sparrow gravel at my feet, this confusion

of the senses, do not shed snake skins' whisperings past your ears.
If you want to Black Bear me back, flesh through my fur, seed me

senseless with your body, burn me out of the forest into the open plains
where I am Wapiti running and running and running, call me from the sleeper

waves, call me from den and hollow knot, out, the she in it all, amphibia,
anima target I am. I ask. Please, just put me out of my misery.

*In the service of life sacrifice becomes grace.*

—Albert Einstein


Let's eat the moonlight's raw sea urchin, run
        out of sleep. To cover our faces
in new green leaves, give
each other the bells of wet earth, we'll
have the probability of hope.

I'll undress in my cranberry thirst, blossom
lilac, you raise the body's temperature,
father our hunger
        to feed outside ourselves.

We will be in the oriole's bright eye. But nothing

can be done to swoon the universe slipping from our sides, nothing
as simple as desire. We shall dream
we are flying the snowdrift praise to the heavens' downdraft.

What I want in me is oncoming. I cannot hide this affliction of light.
        You know it's almost the afterlife, where
everything is unimpressively beautiful. There,
        my body gathers the seed, behaves the season
when all beginnings come
like the translucent hands of the dead
        pressed, still warm, on the forehead
of my lover.

## VENTRILOQUIST'S MASK

> *Ventriloquy*
> *is the mother tongue.*
>
> —Rae Armantrout

My lover...

Fallen, he has, goose-fleshed, into new hive, a colony's
    swarming fifty feet above knit unrolled reams of sky

With a sugared whir-engine sound, a ghost pouring over, held fist over fist fast
    into the air, taking with it my voice too, false every falsetto,
    the very visceral hybrid pitch which has been stolen, extant,

Made of everything passed on, wing-dirge toward an arrow's
    vanishing point, broken voice

To imitate my Icarus wings' stanza against the sun, dissonance of speech,
    my breathing, doubled, feigned to be
    haunted by the same blindfolded echo here perversely heard,

Drone to drone driven by no one I know
    but me, in sleep,—a ventriloquist cadence-played backdraft,
    a wind-old air...can you hear it in the departure?

Face to face, foot in the mouth future dictionary, bloomed tongue, tang,
    ring, this dialect flowering from the head of

The false baritone preacher who prayed for me and me, prayed
    for the overlap tympanum twin language trick, until
    it was too late, this backwards guttural, verbal purblind and

Thrown out wave's aural tremor that's his, his, and is, my,
    marry it, hear it over there,
    invisible body of bees...

*the darkness is nuptial*

—Victor Hugo


       Kingdom's come
to this: night region, wedding complexion
          like walking through fields of dandelion
in the dark
feeling their small feathers dust past
your face,
the ghost-bread, sleepwalker's plain paper dream
with a blind descent down the stairs,
sudden
rain coming towards you, ring of light,
all objects joining hands,—
       darkness again
as unstitched as
the Chinese blue-black and the no explanation-
orange
peeled from its own skin to be sky.
Have you
       forgotten the marriage of more than two
things, separation of self to be
one
in a final lacking of color,
the way thinking appears on a screen
for the doctor,
       the way making love leaves you
stranded
on the image of the body on the bed?
It has dissolved on the skin
       where you'd rather not
say the words for conjugation,
separate the verb
      from the tense
         nor ever harness what happened to you
when night put the lights out
on the tongue.

## ABSENTEE MASK: THE VELVET BIRD

*It's so much better when it's you telling the story.*

—Dai Sijie


and verb,—

Oblivion's lack of speed in the skull    all iambic at the skin burial
and nothing feathers or
felt like this at the onset of seeing into the brain for first time.   Trench
and gray folds.        Widowed like real desire at

this answer for every anesthesia tease
or messenger the sentiment home and taste:        sweet bird, seed bird
I see you from inside, all sides, you
hide speech as in peeled peach, pealed
screech fetched from the throat's ties and nipple-stitched shadow without
a side-glance as answer to

all the King's horses and the King's men
who couldn't bring you back right word's rite, once word of you home
where you have your say aside
me, bitten, married to the idea, a drowning deity, a day of
break and bar-none to the sung
song, say it, song-snug, fit for and fed to hand to mouth, fed
down toward        your hand
and the ampersand bid
for the next despair, a      thinking ladder held up against this

disappearing blue,
the down side of things unremembered here                to
hearsay, yes, he reads my mind, reads your mind, an arm's length
and no further at touch taken, heed        once wing, body-hovered—
and ask me how I feel holding back?            So very here-here in
        vowel over
vowel, that withholding
is the asking price and, of course,     tall order, all

flight of me.

*...With what instrument do we measure*
*the integrity of our minds*
*filled with each other?*

—Forrest Gander


With what, we are
Measureless, inside the undefined space in each other:
    expanse-aria, this hello-paragraph of dreaming
thin air, future air

    burning gold and purple feathers on the horizon,—
some two miles above
    green and brown squares of earth with no boundaries, no cognitive

weight, no country's flag or map pinned with new names. Nothing
    can come close:
        no other recovering sky, no nineteenth century craft,
    no other

kind of undoing
    filling the lungs with oxygen. These heights
    are made for falling, that
apprehension of distance
    but what weightless wash, what turbulent thought

set spinning on its downward rush makes you acolyte to the body?
Unaccounted for in breathing?
    Hover, see for miles, wing and never hit the ground

of your conscious clock, to know where you are going from here.
    Wait and sway, exceed
any dilemma, then open hands, our mouths, wide, to eat wind,

    become weightless as dying
effusive as bees, landless where the generous-erotic century always has us

by the waist. Gravity's pulse baptized upside-down, the horizon's
teeth sinking into our flesh, past jet stream or axis, and
once lifted
we will blue and glitter west
from the northern locus


that we will arouse each other's memory for something
far too blinding and light, ahead:
to walk and walk this blue plank of darkness.

*[Einstein] reasoned that light is radiation; radiation is a form of*
*energy; energy has mass; and mass (the substance of the universe)*
*is influenced by the force of gravity…light has mass and, therefore,*
*weight…*

—William C. Vergara, *Science in Everyday Things*


Understanding this distance, I am always
the invisible line drawn between then and now.
A chromatic god. Don't try to prove me wrong.
I will disappear and reappear without capture. You see,
I am the great frustrater, unruly as an only child with no toy.
Yes, I will outlast any lifetime. Yet, don't you remember when,
Off Alexandria, I was Pharos, the first lighthouse?
I was that deep sea Angler's beam shining without a sun,
the real reason you can live? Call me eternity's
leviathan, the many-eyed messenger and slipknot of the soul.
See my faint novea, my Magellanic clouds, my monster stars,
the curved eye galaxy, night light under the bed. After all,
my science is easily equal to any art, one lie.

It was August once
when the heat carried my body closer, clear across
miles and miles of oat fields. Effortless. The dry crop
raised up like insect wings to my gold air. A singular joy.

Even now, you can still woo my spectral type, sing:
"Oh Be A Fine Girl: Kiss Me" and I will. Remember,
refraction in red, when we were once hinge to each other?
I was better than food in your hands. I would lift and part the dark
for you, carry all the odds when you lost patience.
Such smallness of weight to pay for.
But listen, the black sand pours into the hourglass
of one ear and out the other. Someone's
going to know what I am made of. Someday,
someone will walk on me like water.

# FISH MASK FROM THE WATER

*...a rain of fish did actually occur in 1817, at Appin, in Scotland. It consisted of a downpour of small herrings, a feat that nature repeated in 1830, at Islay, in Argyllshire.*
——William C. Vergara, *Science In Everyday Things*

As if common sense had a vendetta
        to persuade you nothing is as usual
as it seems, that climbing the bone ladder
        from the heart up to the head, or
better yet, from the head down to the heart, you see
        the slave of your logic
using a child's red beach bucket to empty the sinking boat
        that carries you both out
to the center of the Atlantic, where you see the blue Palazzo with women
        wearing white dance to Rossini's *La Cenereatola*
and you see the Loch Ness monster, green hair of Neptune, and you hear
        bagpipes leading the wind; now, a storm is brewing
in your mind, and your bad behavior comes back to haunt you
        like a daily cup of strong tea, like the ambition
of pleasure. But nothing is unnatural if you think about it, if Bible
        or Buddha says so: sky
traded for sea, the shining multitudes of fish bodies
        raining down around you: a live alphabet.
This is the same year we introduce *perpendicular* to the vocabulary
        of architecture, the year Baron
Jons Berzelius discovers lithium. You can almost count backwards
        as if dreaming and then
you are lifted by an air funnel, past the persistence of dawn, past this
        Gaelic word *iasg* (for *piasg*), fish.
This is what you get for not thinking straight.
        Can you blame anyone?
Perhaps it is just the religious life raised-up somewhere from the sea
        and carried to land
in the black body of some cloud, tiny silver herrings
        like so many polished chrome scales
of a god stealing light,—you see them fall, pristine armies driven off
        his back like rain to writhe at your feet, drown
on air. Tonight, you will not know why. Tonight, when you sleep, you will
        breathe water.

*All hands shall be feeble, and all knees shall be weak as water.*

—Ezekiel, 7:17

Unmoored,
she is not bodied-out by his voice
                    but buoyed
as if it came slowly across this distance
of so many dinner guests, lifted
                    the table, tide rising with nuptial salt
rings' fringe


filling the whole house, waist high
with its green water, unfolding water,
forgetting floorboards or cracks, swimming a single stroke
                    for the doors, flume to the attic, flimmering
and closing the fire trap, watering
                    a mirror's sweep as swallowing all objects
in its path, willingly, as one vowel,
or the float of a word: fish eye, oyster, and olive, blood
bearing his name down
                    her spine like the intuitive realm
of thought, margins dissolving, now


                    flowering air from within
this kinetic seal of approval or
whorl down every Southern drain's clockwise turn
                    toward the earth's magnetic core
with semen, ocean, Orion,—water
                    from far inside, to be liquid movement,
her movement turned to be
the body's alliterative answer back
                    in his direction.

## HER SALT MASK

I. Pepper the Salt

*I'd rather see pepper…grow in my garden*

—Horace

Over here, the salt meadow opens a flood window
    until you can't see the bright grass, trespass
salt from the sea
down the soil's center. Brine carriage.
The painter is driven from the table

to paint. Comes back to eat: urchin sauce, orange flower water
olive paste, bread and fig above a purge of stars,
    head of the table in Cassiopeia's Chair with
a crown of bees. Salutary.

She knows and knows the tea is set for two.
The clock always strikes five
when the sky is minted to a pale green
    skin of grape, and the salt pan is set out where she can't see it
or him. This is called the reserved

space where she is lapsed for portrait, a little late to behave
like this. Light builds the boat,
*a tower of salt, against the green pines of the shore…*

But he is not seeded here
    with some part of her, but salted for the ice
winter away. Distance

changes all images.     Paint
tastes like salt. Salt tastes of salt. All
she had to do was see him once.

II. Butterfly Science

*Pliny (A.D. 77) says that when Pompey seized Mithridates's palace he found the prescription for Mithridates's famous antidote against poison, the last line of which read: to be taken fasting, plus a grain of salt.*

—Bergen Evans

Alight in motion, like a going-on short
bloom, yellow-vivid, alone at it's black tip, tipping the scales,
stopping and starting in the immense air
and edge of tree. Like the insomnia of sexuality, stung salt taste
left behind in crying and coupling
or in ice, this ocean dried on pumice rock, sun flares and sulfur-
salt, *salt as wolves in pride...*
The sky snaps out its early salt, Spanish open blue shirt and its fluent
light, saline language new
to her taste buds: motions her from her body: best compound kiss,
half-asleep but thinking this one butterfly is
crush of abstraction he set upon her only she limits to believe.
But given bath salts, poisons, salt lick
and block, to salt flats like abandonment where no earth is cast,
heaven downed,—dissociation
when dissolved. Can salt luck be thrown over passion, the insignia's
flight pattern above her shoulder or head?
White bracket, alibi-craving, swagger-exit and entrance, this insect
makes perfect soliloquy in
thirsty silence, its salt afterlife, sail wing to the wind for her to see,
motion's salt, salt wounded, the sky-sea
rocking her casualty toward him, coming up a half-shadow span, air-
born, where her own salt worth now spills, lands
on Klaus Kinski's face. The butterfly stays vesper and proves no rule
binds rule, *salis grano*, her only skin,
when the real danger here is to pause and to cure what is in her
caught form.

## FACE MASK: THE ART OF PHYSIOGNOMY

> *This is because body language is*
> *composed of iconic signs.*
>
> —T. Szasz, *The Myth of Mental Illness*

To find out

what you actually have become, read of the face's bone, map over map,
and shape, size of cheek, line drawn line, leading

your nature ahead of you (entering you as you speak),
ahead of mouth and *r* of the eye's iris—
black imbedded in the language-telling of your brain—there's more
*purr* in persona, more *descent* in your iridescent tooth's enamel
when you laugh

than the trust lost in the shape of a high brow where
*you'll never see a profound thinker* here, as if thinking were
confessed in the sight of another's countenance,

that the unacknowledged landscape was made to be
climbed, read ear to ear, listened to by
the heart with its cornucopia shaped blood earhorn—or by the hands'

face-up palms, water-like whorls to each of the fingers composing
recognition over the face's features (heavy Braille)—that a soft hat-red and

weak disposition could be cornered in the mouth, at first not seen
but understood like a Master painting's annunciation
stroke over stroke—tell me
a homecoming truth, ( I am answered with a look of hate), or

will you just show yourself in the hard bone-
structure lasting the next life? The nose widens or narrows
destination. The hair falls out.
The face doubles for something else:

*Disparities such as these can doom a marriage.*

*The dogma of the Ghost in the machine.*

—Gilbert Ryle


You have put it on for no one.

The long night is about to get longer.
There's a baritone color to the upstairs rooms, a papered smell of
    birds flying.

Under the floorboards
someone is preparing for eternity, an incomplete
occupation at best.

This is as grateful as you get:

numberless music from the furnace, wardrobe's closed
boundary, the South's cottonfield beds
rising above you in a confusion of goose-down and eyelet.

The cupboards are suddenly crowded
with shattered green glass.
A vine winds the iron staircase, despairing.

You kneel upon an opened book, feel this misunderstood, beside
yourself, bedside-mannered and cautioned to look into a mirror.
    Nothing
disappears faster than the face.   Right now

you are as close as the cold, filling the bathtub
with your white hair, funeral pyre of you set on fire,
the crisp synonym of ashes fallen from your mouth…
There's no conclusion to what one feels.
Hear yourself breathe, because

        You are your own grave company at last.

## DUE NORTH: MASK

*You are now sailed into the north of my lady's opinion;*
*where you will hang like an icicle on a Dutchman's beard.*

—Shakespeare

You knew I had discovered the country
sighted from sea edging out the pale horn of plenty
and sworn rim of the world.
Miracles like this don't happen every day
        in the kingdom of seasons, the severance of will.

Subject to symmetry, deemed
without flight, I take the ticket of the centuries
from both your hands. The surrender
of ten thousand miles
        ahead of you, means me. I am that

greased machinery of heresy and hearsay.
This face carries the commerce
of every salt and habit, this face knows
the clockworked white heavens:
        ice float, flame belt, stray magnetic fields.

I am always unmoored master
because I refuse final orders and, because I am the great illusionist
leading you home, I will betray no one.
        It's all in the perspective of direction.

You would never guess I have been here
all along, before the drift pilgrimages and ships full of lemons
and gold. So, you may want to look for me on the uneasy silver compass
        of a spider web or in the lost hemisphere of sleep.

I will bring you back without asking.
Always in the right direction. Just in case,
before looking the other way, you may just want
to consider me on the chessboard with a crown
        and Norway in my favor.

*Where would Wonderland be without the dogmatic lucidity of the temperamentally unadventurous Alice?*

—Elizabeth Bowen

How many windows can a house bear?
All the legs have tables, all
the chairs, seats, if your lesson is sitting, to be sure...*to grow
to my right size again; and the second thing is to find my way.*
        But the sky is ironed flat here.
        I must risk my table manners
for a purse full of pink candy. I must keep my eye on
everything like a cat, sweet, poor tabby.        Only

I am unmade, out of habit and thinking is no door.
I prefer what the cat perceives, seasonally being of course,
and if that cat can, can you tell me why not can I?
        If it's all the same to you
which it isn't, dear, you being far from where
I can see...Undoubtedly
there has been a mistake. Knowing

my skirts make better skins for flowers,
were these colors wise to my change as fetching
        for spring. Curious comes
all at once you know; twice is too much
for any tea party, and this garden is so confused

        and interrupted, down to the treacle-
bottom of the well. Taste it and it will wake you, havoc
and at a minute or two less than personal.
I ask myself, inevitable to the truth, is this

        the fond moral, the reason doubted as a teaspoon's
silver edge touching my tooth, *click, tick, tock*? OK:
Let's see them let me alone. Let them paint
        the roses royal red. Let them
eat cake. I'll be the one
        to cut out the heart of the Queen.

## BLINDFOLD MASK: QUEEN'S REIGN OF TERROR

*I have a kind of halloween mask*
*Which I am afraid to put on.*

—Charles Simic


My occupied country floats
in the back of my throat when I name it. A ghost boat, gold-red,
no water but the sound of water from my blood. I have to live there
every day in fear of something that comes from myself. No one else
listens to this involuntary exchange between the coming Age of Reason
and the instant. All dreams depict nothing, only my insomnia inside
the heart. So the future is my curfew. Until you come to me. I have no
storm or shore to follow, but Canova's Cupid and Psyche out of a hat,
a kneeling Robespierre licking my wrists and the will to have their heads
on a gold platter. Here. Here it is: with what you don't expect from me,
in a blink, I'll lead the way back from the blind, unawakened lilac walk
in the farm-dark toward who I am. Unafraid now. Running the maze
until you tell me otherwise. I can take all prisoners, and the earth
which is part upside down. But I won't be able to see ahead, yet know,
my love, you are coming to save me from the guillotine, your face,
the hallow darkness, and an invading smell of leaf-smoke still burning
from your clothes.

*It's a wink beyond the world.*
*In the slow rain, who's afraid?*
*We're king and queen of the right ground.*
*I'll risk the winter for you.*

                        —Theodore Roethke

And you too, Sir, I would.

In equal white, so you can't see me at first, twilight wanton and wearied-walking this edge of the field past north's wind like confession of my name in its bird, released for your mouth. Come, close the window of what I see. All the world disappears there in the instant one blue beetle unsheathes out of the water, a frog slides his wet lid closed, and you set your royal seal upon me, sweet incendiary stain overcoming your rose embrace round my heart-skin. Breathing backwards for you, I'd hang my crown on the limb of your nearest tree. But I am slowly dying under the dead fish-gaze of the moon's one underwater eye which returns every month, no answer. Yet I know you are there, snow-wet carrying the wood and bones for St. John's Fire, for a fist of my hair cut by your sword and kissed. I send my watermark thirst. I send a self-devouring feel from the frozen ground, the after-hive and its empty rooms of yellow light-departure. I cannot be any more unmasked than this. To start down and down the old rain staircase, avalanche depth to you, I hear the skull's open sea imprisoned for a sound of your coming back to me. Let me live your motion forward, become inverted by winter from this body, show no fear because simply, I am not afraid.

## MISRULE MASK: THE ABBOT OF UNREASON

*In medieval and Tudor times the director of the Christmas-
time horseplay and festivities, called also the Abbot, or Lord,
of Misrule, and in SCOTLAND the Abbot of Unreason...*


Call me King.

I wear my deep purple well. Best
        unreason's being. Bring in an ideology of flowers and cake,
a range that is devotional as laughter in all bells and toys.
Jangle-riff me.

        I am snuffed Shadow Boxer, your
Puppeteer grinning red curtains back.
I will be your Hobbyhorse
running the black sand of night skies, the gallop
and canter inside your heart. Father
to this kind of play, called upon Ghost, wayside and croon, I
will Bellboy your slant, and there
bite to call me Misnomer, the name
which stumbles from your mouth to mine. Every time

        I will enter the earth upside down, pinch and periwinkle.
Unraveler, or Reveler, I delay and am called. Plums fall
like grackles from the trees. My cockled shape sized to the season, my
thrown anchor dropped into your sea
for a song. And if
the soul's inexorable, so are we. With Kingdom
of hunger and thirst by way of desire, I bring down the Christmas
House, bitter berry for the brew thrown back
in merriment. Much
ado down to our nothingness, sweet.

        Wake. Kiss me under the table.
Let me do my worst... There's a feeling
        here, for hire.

*Trouble, oh trouble*
*Set me free*
*I have seen your face and it's too much,*
*too much for me…*

—Cat Stevens

It is near 20 B.C., a year you were murdered at Lindow Moss in Cheshire England, one religious sacrifice, and now your brown skin, still intact, is preserved by a bog.

*Let low tides breathe between your ribs, before sleep, eyelash*
*the whale's baleen, then wish the purple hydrangea was your hair.*

AD 37–41, you, Caligula, sexually torture and kill at will's ease, once named Caius Caesar Germanicus, and still remember the military boots you wore as a child.

*The cello's body becomes hers, the musical notes, a series*
*of small colored moths sent adrift to lift toward the ceiling.*

You, volcano of liquid fire, gray cinder ash smoke and bellow, Mt. Vesuvius, in one exhale, bury Pompeii and the entire city of Herculaneum: AD 79.

*Red canoes burning candles row out to the mouth of the Dead*
*Sea where ten thousand torsos, not clouds, cross the sky.*

The Plague arrives with you traveling on a flea in Sicily, 1347, killing you and a total three quarters of the population in 20 years, bleeding black.

*The magnolia trees are green with fish, not leaves, hundreds*
*dropping silver scales, rainbow water and oil into the grass.*

You are burned at the stake, feet-first for flames named a witch, now 1400, when you are mother, neighbor, an herbalist healing the sick in a stone coastline village.

*Bees-comb made out of broken church stained glass, pollen, its*
*hive lights up by night, a swinging lantern, music of no wind.*

By 1450, you've become Guttenberg, serving words, aligned by
your new printing press, the book, Bible, God for everyone to read.

*A Plains buffalo, covered in feathers, roams the dining room*
*where you eat a blue plate of seahorse bones and yellow kelp.*

On a sugar plantation in Brazil, a Portuguese owner with a mind for
the slave trade, you mark the year 1510, stand and stand with no hat,
in the sun.

*In the hospital next to you, the sky opens inside her eyes*
*each breath less, grows loose freesia from her chest*

You, Carvaggio, red robed, flee Rome after killing a man in 1606,
never to settle anywhere thereafter, all paintings dreaming ahead of you

*She can't swim the mountain's black water, but twelve gauze birds*
*free from each splash, her mouth a spotted purple orchid, open.*

The 1616 Inquisition stops you with threat of torture and death, Galileo,
in your center of gravity, Copernicus' heresy, and the stellar composition of
the Milky Way free.

*Doll hands litter the darkness under the bed…doll bodies making*
*love to the sound of hard rain, horse-hooves and sandpaper.*

This: 1692 brings you an earthquake's final heave, Jamaica's whole pirate
city of Port Royal falling, you and your pearl necklace, to the ocean.

*By morning the kitchen floor is covered in sea turtles while he*
*picks potatoes which are really light bulbs burning his hand.*

*The problem of shoes demonstrates how the most barbaric things
pass as acceptable through the force of habit.*

—Magritte


Where did you think you were going with that gun?
Indebted and intended to wake you up, *les amantes*, I'll pull your trigger
        first when you least expect it, against
        the missing days, wearing my hat

and black umbrella, my somnambulism the furniture now shares
with me in the house, if they can claim kinship to me
        as you have done, smoking
        yourself down to size.

I'd lick your boots, your breastplate clean, shine your clocks
to come candid: my door is slightly ajar: come inside my outside, seen
        by common sense like a collection
        of missing buttons and body parts

where I roll up my pant legs, walk right into the pleasure principle,
the blood-water, up the ladder of fire, past my prior assumptions.
        Be & be what it may & be
        that brute assertion

I always thought you were. But, for God's sake of habit, take off
your work boots first, set them out on the dining table
        and fill them to the ankle with
        the very best red wine you have.

## IT MASK: HANNAH HOCH AND THE OTHER WOMAN

*...No, that's not what he said. He said, liberates itself in*
*sameness. Then he decided with a heavy heart to abandon the*
*female soul and to devote himself only to chives from now on.*

—Hannah Höch, *Artist*


Think again.

You think you know her each time
you name her, the outcome upon the face constructed,
                    gone to the dogs, her own
        bone to pick with you, little same dance, detour, devotional....


Tribal-orchid came this head and Dada, the skin,
*Fremde Schonheit, strange beauty*
and fiction,—that's how, montage, you'll see
                                her.
See: the body
part for looking. You think
my narrative is entrapment, but who
            made a mask of it, all face?
Who eats or speaks with their eyes closed?
She says (poly-narrative) she is not what you think.

The photos are cut from what is missing and
*the "chapter" man is finished for me*, nothing new or news
            in the otherwise, now
sexuality's hand, a fetishism so complex, the viewer's
brunt has been noted, its *mettle conquering*, always

the free form from me.

> *more fetichism of our luxury goods and gadgets*
> —*Saturday Review of Literature,* 1949

Sweet fetish:

desire's Portuguese, artful and effective in extended
senses, nostrum's medicine magic.
Concealed by this mask's repeating design
        soft blue feather and bauble-glint, all
lack of attention, faux animal fur surround, the outstanding
gold paint over the red
cedar face.

The mask draws you near
enough: I know your skin. Come
closer—I have tasted
this salt before, pushed my tongue out of the mouth
opening, licked the rough edge, known
its shape is more the shape of an eye than an O.  Oh,

put your mouth to its mouth,—it is all I shall wear.
Repeat everything backwards.
*Fetish*  sounds like air escaping through
the birch trees. *Fetish*  sounds
like a circle breaking up, the back
of my hand over your beard. *Fetish*, this parting
of lips but not the teeth…is measure to the rest.

Hold your breath
back, and take my exhale…

## OF MEASURE MASK

*Be why.   They will.*

—Gertrude Stein

And will make more of us
awakening
over   blown hours       clouds' whole girdled forms
round remember       is come
to grow           is measure to the rest, measure
hoe and dark corn       overwhelmed by beetles
bedded out, our
escaped gender there    is
leaving us         leaving us           blood
of nothing but alone-inevitable         generous
whole house flowering vowel
from us, canopy breathing is secondhand time       is instead
a newborn complexion       the feeding world of
no, no, yes
what laws against wonder     make us ask
did the dead on the fingernail breed           is
a wedlocked picture         there is
nobody this ready           than us
no childhood likely     is complete
repeat question's this         and there
fail the ax's North Pole         at
the center of the boat-bottom
will be the water from us
will be the why
will morning all over again
invisible
this way           and will

*If there were a middle     ground between things and the soul*
*or if the sky resembled more sea,*
*I wouldn't have to scold*
                                        *my heavy daughter.*

                              —John Berryman

Will I?
I wouldn't have to scold
the dead father with his hands still          in the air, nor
scold the tiny mother whose fled, frail heart
now beats in my chest.

If the fitful water rose and rose
wrecked by this propositioned summer's swoon, sent
the children on their way
to a future not denied by its distinguished days, an Irish
skunk-drunk sort of business
& homaged just once          dream, then

I wouldn't have to scold
the brother whose garden riddle is bad habit
somewhere I've never seen
or mourned for, its green expanse so
          ordinary.

If the blue that was wagered behind the sky
skewered not one more flower
but bagpiped its loose skin adrift & insane, sad, then
I would not have to
scold my son's eyes'          color or see.

I wouldn't have
to moreover the soul or fever-gape at the common ground
(slower momentums & desperate beauty)
which never had a middle dirt distance, narrative or daughter
like mine          this invisible
heaviness inside unrivaled & I there
too, happy          to say.

## COSMOLOGIST'S MASK: PERSEPHONE

*Right now I think the planet is the constellation Virgo. If we find*
*it, I would like to name the planet Persephone, for Pluto's wife.*

—Dr. Conley Powell


There: my own body is to be seen: anonymous
        as heavenly tease, brilliant
beyond the goddess of love and the blood planet
in Jove's range            (defiant indifference)
past Jupiter's only father
and faith's tawdry patience, a flintlock-light wink.

But what wanderers would
        second guess the facts' significance, or
Saints' mathematics, mirrors and drift prism gases,
the good-natured random objects                (part escape)
I drag along my orbit, round
the blood, down for the count of days?

All you have to do is gaze into the church
        of my face to know I have changed
your early calendar and language, your daily life
as heaven's evidence, just what all the other planets have done.
Indoctrinated by sky, by the helm of the galaxy, and
absent-minded as Newton's windmill, I am            (Proserpine)
invented by what you discover next. You see and see,

I can sing any song over in five languages,
        disgrace the table covered in candles, toss my red hair
into oncoming snow. Who earns my name ignited by seeing,
unlabeled hunter, Delta Gemini's missing X, tenth planet
you believed in all along, beloved, being dependent?
O, brief absence, bright eye pinned to the universe…
destiny will breathe its icy breath down my neck.
This circle: all reason currents past.            (by my wrist)

That I'll lay down your French days of the week
        and book of hours,—contrast choice for you,
wherein spring chasms will open and open on their own.
I'll take my chances with Adonis until then.   (Flowers resurrecting )
I'll roll pomegranate seeds from my tongue to yours, in time. Yes,
I'll take my chances and ghost a nubile glance every century,
back in your direction, if you'll still have me, or better,
if you can find me.

## PHANTOM MASK: MERCURY

*There has not passed a single day (in the previous thirty years),*
*without the Sun being explained, drawn, or photographed in Italy,*
*England, Portugal, Spain, America, France and elsewhere. That*
*the supposed (intra-Mercurial) planet has never been seen means*
*that it is either well-hidden, or it does not exist.*

—Camille Flammarion, 1890

There's not a day you do not know me.
Not a place elsewhere than here, where I am hidden from
your thinking, tireless as your breathing, far
beyond anything exempt
of patience, fallible, more pleasing than gravity under your feet. Feel
me being foolish for you, fiery as you want, wheeling obediently
around the sun. I receive seven times more light
than you, more heat and hard luck.
Courage comes

                    unforeseen in ticking fractions, dividing
and dividing and devising this sweet disorder outgrown
from a field of stars planted
blind on your foreheads. I can raise the stakes, mind
no one's manners but my own, out-harvest
what is harrowing. You say

                    you'll be my brother, my brotherhood
of dry land, narrow misses and motion, never too late to catch my warp-
eccentric orbit, without prejudice, to tell me
nothing shy of desire, you'll have an ornate
waist to wrap around, Aristotle's dream-cast, nothing
you would deny yourself under the circumstances.

                    The infinite faces looking upon me ask
for guarantee that I am really part of the galaxy's scheme, call out
what they heard in your one good ear, until the wide-rocking
you back to yourself says *this*
was just another way to greet the darkness
when it knows you are coming.

60

*It was a popular medieval belief that paradise, a land or island
where everything was beautiful and restful, and where death and
decay were unknown, still existed somewhere on earth. It was
usually located far away to the east and in the 9th century maps
it is shown in China, and the fictitious letter of Prester John to
the Emperor Emanuel Comnenus states that it was within 3 days
journey of his own territory—a "fact" that is corroborated by
Mandeville. The Herford map (13th century) shows it as a circular
island near India.*

*—Brewer's Dictionary of Phrase & Fables*

Indeed. For you are invisible as an undiscovered island
and ready to rehearse for the end
which is a sickly sweet
nothingness whispered
into everyone's ear, the fuchsia
elsewhere you long for, blue
at the end of the barometer, and the lasting
grace of green rising around you, glittering.
It must be true. Your heart still depends on it,

granting you this:
Paradise exists, the between-world
you want so badly, contagious
and proven by word of mouth, just
a smooth stepping stone-throw
away from here.
This, this is

the planted seed in your mind's black eye
or call of the wild at
the lid of Pandora's box.
This is stopped time
cupped in the mouth of a calla lily, withdrawn
denizen's milk-dream from death, Nirvana's
underside, Cornucopia's compass

the size of Texas, and after that, the circle
you fall into
to save yourself from drowning
or from making the simple mistake that all else
will faithfully end
                no further than here.

*I think I never*
*slept that night. I only dozed. And ranted.*

—Gerald Stern

And then suddenly you are forty
and you want to take out the little pocket knife
the one with a red rabbit's foot attached, and you want
to peel your own skin and call out in the darkness
to no one in particular since the body temperature rises
with each thought, and the sounds outside enter your gut
like red pepper, sounds that by now have moved on up the street
with a tail of leaves and candy wrappers made for children screaming
in the car, made for the time you forgot what you wanted
to say and happened to look below on the pavement running
its white and gray knuckles down your imaginary spine,
and you said to yourself—*that* is what time does, that
is where it goes—only to catch your breath
for you when you least expect it and when someone
you love expects nothing more of you
as if the self has lost its mother memory in the movie theater
and like Swiss clockwork your hands had to touch
your face just one more time to be sure how far
you have come, out of the suspended hive of desire,
out of the kingdom of strangers with the blood
pressure of dreaming, the soaking sheets
and graveyard hair, the whiskey breath shoes and shine
of water glasses, all the while telling yourself it will be OK,
a Vivaldi's season, all the while not wanting
anything else but to be conscious, awake
when field lightning counts down the days
leaving glowworms and aftersex behind,
the full jacket of terror that you might have missed
something, perhaps the ghosthair of dust moving
under the bed or decaled words pasted on your tongue
while you squandered the petty cash of holding back,
your hands held down in the icy water,
there, at the mouth of a winter carp mistaking
your finger for a piece of food, the last food
God had intended for some other fish.

63

# SERMON MASK TO HERSELF

*She would not even let him come through the door, which*
*a moment later she had to close because the house was filled*
*with yellow butterflies...so many butterflies that she could*
*scarcely breathe.*
—Gabriel Garcia Marquez

Or, I'd gladly make space
for you, love, with this one move, throw
off the psyche-scent
for the god-dogs, send proof
of existence pledged in light, its innuendo
of wild lemon and road ice.      I'd get everything
I want and my own way
without the rumored embroidery of absence
because I am here, approximate
amorphous distance run its course

to keep coming back again.      Walk with me.
The woe and dotage
of humanity sealed on these lips like a first kiss
lacking gender, like a hit
from a truck's tailpipe in nobody's garage,
is yours.
But winter draws its fixed circle
above your head
when you hear me come, all pronouns and possession.
Good kind of guilty

I give back.            Be
bushwhacked into thinking like me.
Sweet, licked skinflint kind of girl behind the open dry
fields, still failed for
the refrain, in this house, this sacred workplace
made for the god of you, yes
you there, for you
lacking obedience, for you, a failing-blue bedroom full
of yellow butterflies,

            dear.

# ELLIPTICAL SPEECH: MASK: A LETTER TO PEN NAME

*"I grew up with a lot of punctuation myself, so I can understand your nostalgia for parentheses," the dashing Sister Ka exclaimed...*

—Harryette Mullen

Dear Pen-Name,

I am wild with poker and the odds are in someone else's favor. The flavor of cowry shells, of ice chip just out of its box. Cistern-smell. It makes me all the livelong dog-tired and ready to give up myself. Yes, I am aware the sky is mirror, the predecessor to dream. Just one more go and I might win. Win back the predictable weathercast, foreplay and longshot's ying-yang. Win back every lost friend and the feeling for right words. But that's hoax, the hogwash trough we fill. We are all on the warpath to nowhere there and given another minute up. This is not just fan mail genre, but the cut and dry, the rival faith. A small price to pay, don't you think?

Counting out loud, you can devote your dynamic to me. I have been told before, the root result is a good one, a sure bet. The next move you make may be mine. Because payday preserves freedom. Because money and short kisses recycle, idle the same water round the planet which figures as one. Own your anger. Sardine the kitchen with hype and salt. I say that in earnest. Honest. And every day. My assonance is passionate as your silence. I am in love with spoons. Oh, overture famish! You must be able to see me as I say this. Probable as no number. Errored in distant cosmology, numerology. From my face, quickly losing the luck of the present tense.

I will prevail your wise reply.

## ARTIFICE IS ENOUGH: MASK

*Truth is entirely and absolutely a matter of style.*

—Oscar Wilde


For every white noise there's a washing machine and the dead weight
　　　　of your name being pushed around.　　Mirror in your mouth.
There's an incurable look in the eyes, the French bridegroom of admiration
for you.　　Not everyone

digs their own grave. Some people just like the feel
of the shovel, the funerary smell of loose
　　　　　　　　　　　　　　　　　earth, art of the face.
I'll tell you what: I'll pick your brain for just a few extra coins.
I'll be your fairy tale of tall stories and dark chocolate apples left
　　　　　　　　　　　on your pillow.　　I'll be the child crossing
　　　　　　　　　　　the street you never saw

in the blue & blind eye of memory.
I'll even take you to lunch in an amusement park made for poverty.
We'll eat everything that moves, even the trapped birds
of our own hands.
I'm fête for the unintentional, yes.

　　　　　　　　　　Can you blame me?

*I wanted to marry an absence,*
*The sound of stars crumbling without any malice*
*In a corner of the universe*

—Thomas James

Take my scrubbed face first


      though that has nothing to do with it, my weight and lack
of tolerance to booze,—take my giddy blood
before
      you enter and leave my body. Take

the girl trapped in her neighbor's cedar sweater trunk
      the one wearing boy's clothes, impatient as a peony. Take
      the descending

breath, the whole house closed like a ribcage for the rains, and take away
      the commotion of wallpaper and broomstraw, the lost importance
of money, now

            the green pyres of silkworm's leaves,—
      and you can take my veins' blue
                        slipstream from the heart

raised up to your needle
where I'll be collapsing like an origami star into myself

disappearing from all abacus circumstance
                  a captive stone

for the vanishing duration no one understands. Take


the rusty hinge of childhood, the fields
      of ash stinging my eyes, like the withering light, take

the swinge and belling of my voice talking on its own worshipful
gratitude, the new ledge

                    of snow from my hands
                              and Limoges teeth from my bones, take

the colored scarves from my throat
                    all my accidents of longing unearthed

and bled on the tile floor, belly, whittled and opened, fished for
off the coast of the invisible forgiveness,—take the part of me




                                        already damaged and dissolving
at this absurd speed from childbirth and sex,

the pulse of poppies pressed down hard
                    on my wrists, take everything imperfect

so I can use up all the sterilized air around me, fall

                                        and come back
                    to myself, the way I should be, a little less.

*I recall the rosetree that sprang from my breast.*
*I recall the myriads of birds in the cage of my head.*
*I recall my third finger the branch of the myrtle,*
*I recall the imprisoned women wailing in my bowels.*
*I was the figure of the Surrealist Exhibition*
*With the mask of roses face…*

—George Barker

Face first, unfailing, frail, the mask is a step back from thinking. No one blooms until someone else responds. See, like so many small red fists, but softer, like my love's opened sex. Before-sleep roses. Petals' weave one wave at a time, not me, me. Flesh of my skin reenacted in an outburst of red and lavender. Embroidery bloom, the unearthed face and then the buried face, mourned for. The first blossoming, as in beginning, stopped by blush being seen, blossoming to be plant again, all breathing. To take up the air in the room. After-impression coloring the gaze, perfuming the passing glance, the mask will wither. I am what might happen, the subjunctive mood everyone wants to be in. If truth be part garden, grown along the path, short-lived. Implied in silence, withering, I, too, am unexpected by you, mask of new pleasure not lasting. Opening. See my mistaken, mask of me, fisted head now seeing you? Alone with my rose, little consequence by any other name, carried by this face, so many roses for beauty, mixed Dog with fiction, written into history for many a king, queen and one Mary, Moss, Daily, China, Musk, Burgundy, White, Infidelity Yellow and in the extant version, here in a gallery of onlookers, plain. See with the eyes, see with a question, with a hand that nothing induces it to seize, such mediocrity, masquerade, mine. Thorn to thorn. Transformed, I am not transformed but what you knew all along. Now: flowery kingdom of the face, rose mask made for a world of mixed messages. To desire to press mine to yours! Skin/petal, petal/ skin. To lean with the light. Smell. Roses face to your face. Dust to dust. And a room disappearing. To lose this, thinking, my human means.

# MASK OF FLOWERS

*When a flower is given, the pronoun* I *is implied by inclining it to the left, and the word* thou *by inclining it to the right.*
— *The Language of Flowers, 1884*

Am I hurrying this way through the hothouse of sky to see you again, tailspin
through the compliant brothels of pollen unleashed and flying to this occasion

of saying good-bye—the giving here and the good-bye like a pale blessing
of cut irises set down in their water, their resting place? We can't go back:

there's only one earth, unearthed. Poppies and purple lupine become
endangered, voracious as underwater song, but my earpiece tells me

not to take you back to the beginning of the story: I am already diffident
toad-plant, milkweed arcade, woodbine or insolvent and as sure as

an engraved invitation brought in by heady wind of valerian. You
would have thought I had no voice in the matter, no hand-outs, nothing

left to breathe,—but look at me, night-picking bracts and anise, missing
mint bodice: postmark of stone-buds and the yellow witch's broom index.

I am told you will survive with the expressionless narcissi,
arranging yourself, mignonette, like an ampersand on a lack of sleep,

that you will believe in yourself out of context. But that can't be so, saving
green grace of one planet, one face at a time taken. I have taken the daisy

chain too far, toppled the lavender rose heads for a tyrant or two, even
shaken from the fable of passionflower and midnight weed throughout

an azalea-lament, the deadly oleander gate. It might have been different
once, with complexion of goldenrod and open flux of orange osier like

fish bait for the moon's white sulfurous orchid to reign over us.
Now the hooded monks have returned devotion to the forest floor

and I am thinking you will ploughblade out of your paint box,
saffron-stained, bearing one lily,—you will come pollen-close, see

the gingersnap and cane-break, burn marks of autumn's inclining, see
me, see for yourself, what still outgrows over here, a little to your right.

*The English version of "Cinderella," originally translated from the French by Charles Perrault, contained an error that was never fixed. Perrault translated* pantoufles en verre *(glass slippers) instead of* pantoufles en vair *(squirrel fur slippers).*

—Jane O'Boyle

You must know my proximity to the animals first. See for yourself. Every time a crumb falls, the mice know. Other small creatures gather seeds and replant before night. There are fields of unpicked Georgian cotton for me. Deep water white pearls in my mouth. The sound I make is volatile's abuzz and a stubborn spondee follows behind my carriage. Hear *le petit mort* under these floorboards of earth. That is how I know I am alive. See, I am retreating into kisses: *Bonne Bouche.* But how could you anticipate me, such artifacts? I am a closet thinker. I fulfill my duties but not for all the housework in the world would I give up this secret. Understand, I have a *mind of winter*, I do. But there are whole days I forget myself. So, every day, I beget a dare. I sew a patchwork of full-blown grammar just for you, an unfolding avian gesture when I move. To begin another fiction, I replume without color. This is my maw, my musk-proposition. What you cannot see. Even the cow lilies breathe for me. There's still a chance spring will bring back memory. I'll spread my chimney ashes in the surrounding flower garden. This insurrection of joy will never end. I can circumflex the next minute made by having no sex because love has never been a consequence. Yes, I'd like to keep my feet warm but I am terrified of shoes…

So, I remain faithful to death since it's the only straight promise I have. I work for it, walk until it hurts and burns. I don't have to cut my red hair or bathe, and eating has become mathematical: as if time talked back in light swatches, crickets ticking the thickets and as if my skin was banished to the present tense impression that nothing changes here. All measure is always circumference. I can pull out the bright baby teeth, every star from its sewn black mouth to make an infeeling fairy tale lie for you. This is my forest now, the green rat's maze made by me. There's much more ground to cover. The forest becomes thinking which becomes a circle and thinking becomes sleep and sleep becomes the furnace someone else falls into. The circle becomes Hansel but Hansel had nothing to do with it. Even together, we never seem enough. Nothing ever seems enough, so when I get there, clearing the stolen bread seeds from my pockets, when I come to myself and she comes back to me, then I'll know, all the way down the spine, how this blood-distance betrayed my name.

## SHE MASK: INVERSION

*I had my luck, I met a lovely monster,*
*And the story's this: I made the monster me.*

—Charles Simic


Her name has always been bad
                    chime and tremble, the drum-
pomegranate anemone in the blood, my seed-wind, keeping keyboard
averages between
                    black and white. Outside.

Impersonator with no mercy, zealous seaweed-breed,
                              proximate host to my bygones, on
the chance for misfortune, she's half-naked
                              for a swan-song, for
a bedside letter with no manners.
Honestly,
        I'm not dreaming though it suits me. You see,
        she's baited to be me: devourer
        of attention. She's right here, brooding the shape of fish.
        This version

always swerves apparent:
                    She could be koi, saltwatered and retrieving O's for air,
                    tied with cat-gut to the rust anchor, strung-out on the last
                    happiness, white sand filling her ears. Now


you can hear the sound
of the ocean approaching. Midway,
                            the self has to
sweat it out. So, I stand
on shore, crowded by miscarry and blunder.
Deemed everlasting, she's posturing
for a chance to be forgiven, but I cannot say her name
                                    out loud

74

because it was me and not my amusement making it up.
How red tides distance themselves to descend shelves.


    This life

    just wants to begin again
    with an embrace, but she will
                keep me from 'I' as long as she can.

Don't understand. Farewell, farewell…

        I know I belong inside.
        But this

      is where I do my best thinking.

## QUEEQUEG'S TATTOOS: A HEADLESS MASK

*He speaks a farewell kiss to me.*

—Bob Dylan

*Pagan psalmody*
singing his checkered face into my sleep, tomahawk at our side,
head in the bag. Ready
            to venture out against the colorless light,
slandering a white gaze.

That's all it takes to find the world on
           its bow, turn a wheel against the waves.
You are asking for rain, offspring cloud and fish
trapped inside the blood. Overrun
by no one's desire. Alone.

Finger the first domino
    and kiss the tail of who I am
underwater. Cannibal, harpooner we all are. And her: her

alchemy goes unnoticed thus far, for *all deified Nature*
*paints like the harlot* where the clock's run down
to the heart's weight

           to the weather we look for.

*We prefix so significant and infidel a word*
until it becomes ours,
hearing the earth's meant-metronome silt,
one name at a time, one word translated into so many
           black squares on a face.

But I never cared what I looked like, nor her, nor
him. It's true, the past is checkered. Tattooed. Permanent.
Leviathans

and men, let's go ahead, ride it like an argument
of who we are until we sink
with the *god-bullied hull*
                    into the next six thousand years
of water.

## MASQUE

*Her face kept swallowing itself.*

—Susan McCabe

I, I never held anything personal
Against you. There are at least two of us here, so come
Carnival-close, my misprint alias caught inside the Book of Names,
Motile, mine, mime and mummer running the numbers at night, my
Push-over elegy edged-out, my perfect imprisonment velvet
Mask, *M. Marchiel* in iron mask, my 1703 black face, postponement
To fate and hood-wink, oh, you can talk back, back-talk, my lux,
My chicken wishbone caught in the throat-open mask, my
Self-consciousness masked from me, cast to plaster object in error,
Body-double doubling the odds against us, set to music, two-
Faced, maybe three, my flush crawl space in the mind
Where, *Ich Dien,* I serve, am iamb slang-maid made to make you
Sing my by-word, nay-word, password dance into the next
World, masquerade insult-sworn to the lips, therapy's gas mask-
Oeuvre, power in temperament, my only stunt-
Double over the white cliff, honestly, bully at the rosewood
Pulpit, what, what do you think of me, make of me
In the skull, that gray nunnery we try to escape

From, or are you the mirror-confinement
Covered in tattoos, camouflaged and fledged for fallen leaves,
Exhale-faced feigned to be me, my imperfect history, clam-digger
For a bad, wet dream, claim-digger with this face-weight in gold
Restored to the ancient gods, perhaps that Pharaoh's rat face rubbed
In scarab oil feeding the mongoose, do tell, dear freed helot,
Vanquisher in Voltair's French, icon, *et ux,* who you are
When the day changes its time and your Fair Maid,
Spontaneous combustion, Ignis Fatuus burns green, close
To the ground, when I take my face-lift float in a pool of light
In order to see you, or deeper my disguise, take my diving
Helmut, snorkel mask holding its minutes of darkness,
Forelock of seaweed and cockle blood laid out, seaglass teeth lost,
My underwater air spent here, my ass, mere ink re-print

Fool on these brass cast oath features scaled down to size,
Underscored and scorned, this plaster mask reverse in virtú, or
I'm not like that, I'm like this picture not seen, this
Skein, Phaedra piercing the skin of myrtle
With hairpins, walking and walking and walking over
The eyes of the needles who wink back at us, see
Our false face, vizard, visor, the faker flour-flush fraud just

        For you, that third person we keep on hand, on
Deck, in the hall boot closet, worn-out in conversation, in
Inversion to the perceived, the poem who shovels the face,
Knows you, so many of us really, you and me, muddied, my incognito
Repeated fuck unfolded like a dusk kimono covered in birds, like
The deaf hands of the dead working your bent biblical ribs,
That perfect insult spit-out, swallowed, savored and savored
Simply because it's hard to believe and breathe this riddle
Because all the centuries are ours when the argument has passed
And we recognize the mask is real, stealing what
We already know, my pirate eye, myself ecstatic and mad,
Our teal green parrot passing the sunset shriek, my best cliché
Shorn sad and good-mothered at the pearl, seated
To be at the window, at the stranger's embargo cargo of last light
In the eyes, carried on your breath when you break the back
Of who I am over your knees, when you show faith in
Lesser gods, you, also prayed to, swooning aloft my makeshift, shape-
Shifter in the attic of loneliness, language-angst and art, axe
Swung at nature's bright-in-exile head,—do you understand
This, my squeaky hinge, very hindsight of hearing your name
Behind me, head over heels down the stairs persona, fall-out
Sickness when in front of me, facing me like epitaph, your long-lost
Love's worst nightmare comes pageant-true, your favor fevering urgency
And asking birthright reels when the cork-ballast of this heart goes out
To sea, so do please save me, boil the blue egg of the world on the face for me,
Offer what the body has to offer as expression, accidental DNA, danger's
Ekphrastic silence tasted as green, my plea, my pledge, wanting, my bargain
At the upended, scratch-end of the day in perpetuity, mask, masque,
Feathered, outright, and salted, held so beautiful you can't even see it
        Until it looks back, to be you, there, there,—to see you.

*masks are the order of the day*
                                —Sylvia Plath


**Mask,**
face or head covering used for disguise or protection—
Masks have been integral to drama in East and West, particularly
ORIENTAL DRAMA and the COMMEDIA DELL'ARTE


**Masque,**
courtly form of dramatic spectacle popular in 17th cent. England.
Characterized by the use of masks and the mingling of actors and spectators,
it employed pastoral and mythological themes, with an emphasis on music
and dance.
                                *-The Concise Columbia Encyclopedia*


*...two mythical parts of a single self: the corrupted person who
acts, and the ingenuous soul. The Latin word persona, from
which the English word "person" derives, means the mask
worn by an actor. To be a person, then, is to possess a mask.*

                                —Susan Sontag

*It Mask : Hannah Hoch and the Other Woman*

Dada collage artist Hannah Hoch was the principle triggering influence in my wanting to write this book. The title "Knife in the Kitchen Sink: Perspective Mask" pays small homage to Maud Lavin's book, *cut with the kitchen knife / the weimar photomontages of hannah hoch.* I was preoccupied with the nature of identity-doubling, the opposition of selves rendered, and of the compromised, yet empowering voices of the speaker, the spoken to, and the third, other-consciousness-voice. Her montages, with kaleidoscopic effect, take-in projected resemblances, spectator, persona and seeing oneself, all at once. Lavin writes, "Hoch's use of irony, caricature, the grotesque, and other critical strategies point to an underlying anger that, coupled with the pleasure of repeating some mass media images, opens up for the viewer emotional tensions between anger and pleasure in exploring questions of identity and femininity. But the utopianism Hoch associates time and again with the representations of the New Woman remains alive." It is those principle identity 'dislocations' which occupy the tone in many of the masks.

It became apparent I needed to have an epigraph for every poem, a doubling of voice to voice contact, a call, a response, an echo... a copulative experience between the familiar and the stranger.

*Her Salt Mask*

This poem couples memory of a love with a meditation on the butterfly's unhinging movements and the word origins of salt; I had to include that marvelous moment in Werner Herzog's documentary, "My Best Fiend," when the butterfly lands on Klaus Kinski, causing a shift in his awareness of himself, therefore, also instigating for those of us watching, an immediate suspension of time.

> *a tower of salt, against the green pines of the shore...*
>
> —Octavio Paz

> *salt as wolves in pride*
>
> —Shakespeare *Othello III, iii*

*Sex Mask*

A Tantric-linguistic attempt at writing about sex, without writing about it. In the throws of it, I had not realized I used "enallage." —thank you Baron!

## NOTES

### Magritte's Mask

It seems every one of my books must have a Magritte poem; he certainly understood man's principle tendency to misrepresent himself and what he perceived; to misinform is another way of seeing.

The phrases "missing days," "pleasure principle," and "ladder of fire" are taken titles from his paintings.

### A Weightless Mask: Light

The song reference "Oh Be A Fine Girl: Kiss Me" was actually created by astral-physicists to be used as a format they could remember in order to read spectral codes.

### Mask of Marie Antoinette

"I am calm as one always is when one's conscience is clear" is taken from Marie's letter to her sister, prior to her execution, in response to the fabricated accusations of treason and among other horrific things, sexual abuse of her children.

### Muse Mask Talking: Cannibal

The muse as both a mythic and personalized figure functions here also, as both cannibal and sexual predator, a personified force that mimics what the writer feels about himself and about his/her writing process. The address then becomes, as in so many of these poems, a self-devouring, mirroring self-address, too.

NATURA...6. the female pudenda; 7. the male organ of generation; 8. God. —*Italian Dictionary* by Davenport and Comelati, London

### Mask: Her Cinderella to Her Gretel

*a mind of winter,* —Wallace Stevens

### Phantom Mask: Mercury & Cosmologist's Mask: Persephone

Rather than one Biblically story-driven God residing the heavens, I imagined these planets as beings, one of many gods resisting Camus' "benign indifference of the universe."

*Misrule Mask: The Abbot of Unreason*

The phrase 'bitter berry for the brew thrown back' echoes Edna St.Vincent Millay's "I'll be the bitter berry in your brew yet" and earmarks the dark tone set for the reveler.

*Ghost-Afterlife Mask*

Carphology--a delirious fumbling with the bedclothes

> *...about acts of language indicating what they can't embody.*
> *(Bodily acts suffer the same sorrow, a mortal metric) And it is*
> *in this sense that acts of language too are acts of elegy.*
>                                                   —Heather McHugh

*Moon Mask*

Varuna, in Hindu mythology, shines at night and is linked with the moon. He is represented usually as a white man riding on a sea monster who orders the seasons and controls the rains.

*Necropolis War Mask: A Bearer of Two Faces*

This poem was influenced by the politically-committed southern fiction writer, Thomas Jeffrey Vasseur, his novella on Vietnam, in Malololailai or *Discovering the World* (re-printed as *Touch the Earth*, Mercer University Press).
Then, one hast to be compelled to speak out against what this current government is doing, violating our country and our youth in Iraq.

*Queequeg's Tattoos: A Headless Mask*

All italicized lines are taken from Herman Melville's Moby Dick.

*Masque*

A final rant of address: you meaning me, and all other nouns, pronouns and phrases devised for us, and other than us, to exhaust. Thinking of Stevens' phrase, 'as of two people,' the poems serve as two to three minds, ask for self-reflexive entropy, a reason to experience the fragmentations of self, a discursive movement outward. This poem embarks on the fevered devotion to the subject:

> *The blooming and the mask*
> *Were being alive, an incessant being alive,*
> *A particular of being, that gross universe.*
> —Wallace Stevens

How many have spoken of this self-reflexive motion of the mind? Gaston Bachelard spoke of "the non-I that protects the I…where an immemorial domain opens up for the dreamer." Also in an essay, Lyotard once said, "There can be no work of art if the seer and the seen do not hold one another in an embrace." Yes, yes. In this urgency of being, I value "there is a variety of conflict and collusion," as Oliver Sacks writes in *The Man who Mistook His Wife for a Hat*, that one can be driven to "identity-delirium." Oh but, "we want to become who we are" Nietzsche insists unflinchingly.

> *No more masks! No more mythologies!*
> —Muriel Rukeyser, *The Poem as Mask*